Severe Mercies

A journey of faith, love and mental illness

Judy Bibbins

D1301887

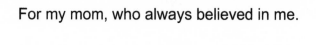

For my mom, who always believed in me.

Preface

For most of my adult life I have battled depression. That's how people phrase it, they "battle" depression. Every day is a battle in an ongoing war. I don't know if anyone ever wins the war, but people do lose. And we hear about it when they do, especially if it is someone famous. The media is always quick to tell us when someone famous takes their own life, but we rarely hear about it when someone is winning the battle. If we hear about someone battling depression, we tend to sit back and wait until we hear the news of their suicide, of them becoming another statistic. Then it will be all over the news: the statistics, the medications, how many people deal with this, etc. It will be the flavor of the week until something else happens to replace the headlines. But what if someone decided to share how they are winning the war? That's what this book is about. How I am winning the war…. without medication.

Most books about depression tend to be, well, depressing. This is a success story, and it's not over! I hope to keep it honest and informative but mostly I hope it offers another perspective on dealing with what is one of the most common mental illnesses of our time. In fact, it is so common that most people have become complacent about it. Antidepressant medication is so common that there are very few people who don't know someone taking some form of it. It's like aspirin or allergy medicine, except you can't get it over the counter. Doctors prescribe it all the time and say there really aren't any side effects, no problems with taking it long term, etc. Does that make it okay to keep taking? I questioned that and this is my story of how I came to the decision to fight "naked." It is a story about my journey, my successes, my failures and, mostly, my faith in God.

Now, for the disclaimer, I have to say that this is not a guaranteed process for everyone. Medication has a place in our society and in fighting mental illness; each person has to choose their own weapons. This story is about what is working for me. It may work for others; I believe that with all my heart. That's why I am sharing it with you. Please read it with an open mind and an open heart.

Chapter One:
Seeds

We are vessels, clay pots, in the hands of God. And every pot has its flaws.

God has chosen to deliver His eternal gifts to the world through such vessels.

He may have to break down and remake us from time to time but use us He will…. with our permission.

He only requires that we gratefully submit our beings and bodies for His use and consecrate our efforts and energies for His purposes.

Rev. Peter Lovejoy

I'm not sure how old I was when Rev. Lovejoy gave the sermon the excerpt on the previous page is from. I wasn't that old, a teenager for sure. And, admittedly, not an age when I was particularly paying attention to the sermon. Don't get me wrong, I loved Rev. Lovejoy and I have many good memories from his time at our church. I just didn't really focus on the message in church at that time. But something about that part of his sermon stuck with me. Sometimes a phrase just speaks to my heart and I hear it differently. I believe that's because God is actually saying it to me, and I need to pay attention.

After the service that day, I asked Rev. Lovejoy for a copy of that part of his message - and I have held onto it for years. My original copy is faded and fragile now, so I have rewritten it several times. Every time I pulled it out and re-read it, I would hear God's voice in it again, but I couldn't figure out why it touched me the way it did. So, in the words of one of my college professors, I "let it incubate." Recently, I stumbled on a copy I had rewritten in calligraphy. (I went through a phase where I wrote anything "special" in calligraphy to preserve it) and I knew that the incubation period was over. It was time to write about it.

I love the imagery of God as a potter, remolding us into what He intends for us to become. And, unlike us, He has no time limit on when we are to become what He intends. He just keeps working on us, adding gifts, breaking us down, building us stronger, showing us how to live to bring Him glory. The key, I have learned, is in that excerpt from Rev. Lovejoy's sermon: with our permission. We must submit to Him, be willing to let Him mold us, show us what He intends for our lives and receive His love and grace to learn how to pass that on to the world.

It is not easy to submit; it goes against our very nature. But when we do, He rewards us with such peace and joy that it changes how we see everything. And what I have learned most recently is that what I have struggled hardest with in my life is the very thing He has blessed me with to draw closer to Him, to see Him more clearly and to share that gift to draw others in. I have a gift to deliver to the world within me, and it is my story. I hope that it helps even one person to see the strength and beauty of God in our darkest moments and to know that they are never alone.

Anyone who has spent any time watching or helping things grow knows that seeds come in all shapes and sizes. It is hard to look at a dandelion spore and a coconut and see them both as seeds, but they are. Some seeds need very little soil or water to take root and grow and can withstand even the harshest weather. Others need to be planted deep and left in the darkness of the soil for an awfully long time before they can take root and begin to grow. Each seed is part of God's design and a miracle of life in its own way. We are only obligated to not hinder their growth, help them if we can, and see the gift within unfold before us.

My parents planted the seed of faith in me as a child. We were raised going to church every Sunday, helping with church fundraisers like the Christmas Fair and Saturday night suppers all summer long. My family served the church - it was a part of who we were. In the Congregational tradition, we were baptized as infants, attended Sunday School, received our children's Bible in fourth grade and were expected to attend confirmation classes at fourteen so we could take our place as members of the church. My three older siblings and I all participated in our summer day camp and youth retreats. Our social life, as a family, revolved around church activities. Even our summer camping trips were with other families from the church. It created a shared bond in that community that has impacted every part of my life. I return to those memories and the lessons learned from my childhood more and more as an adult.

I think I do that more now because I have spent so many years trying to get back to who I was back then - the fearless little girl who laughed and talked with everyone and knew exactly who she was. I'm not saying my childhood was perfect - no one's is and we tend to focus on the best parts of our memories - but even the challenges (my lisp, being bullied) all made me stronger and determined, and I lost that somewhere along the way. I was smart and clever and funny and creative. At some point, that little girl got swallowed up in the darkness of depression and was buried so deep that I almost forgot she existed. But she does still exist.

I believe the excerpt from Rev. Lovejoy's sermon was a seed planted very deep in my heart. A seed that God would use when the time came - and His timing is always perfect.

I think that every time I came across that writing from Rev. Lovejoy, something in me knew I was just checking on the seed. But God would whisper, "Not yet, child" and I would put it away for another time. This last time that I found it, I felt God say, "Yes, now this seed is ready. Make it grow."

The roots of that seed have reached the little girl buried deep within me and she has given her permission for God to rebuild her. She is still climbing out, but she is ready to come back into the world and share her story. This story is my journey and I only ask that you reserve judgement and

I pray that it will touch you in some way and bring you peace.

Chapter Two:
My Garden

I hear voices. That's not something that most people would admit. But maybe that's part of the problem. If people weren't afraid of the looks, or worse, the labels, maybe it wouldn't be so bad to admit when something is off in our head.

So, I'm admitting it. I don't know how to describe it exactly, I think it's voices, but I can't understand them. It's more like a muffled or mumbling kind of sound. I'll be lying in bed, watching television and then turn it off to go to sleep. But I can still hear it. It's like it's in the next room, or outside. And that's what I tell myself - that it must be something outside. Because admitting, even to myself, that it's in my head is too frightening. I don't know if it's in my head, but I don't listen to it. I push it out, try to make it stop, focus on something else until I can't hear it anymore. It doesn't happen every night, but when it does, I need to make it stop any way I can.

I'm afraid of what I might hear if it actually made sense. I know there are demons in my head; I fight them all the time. And I have for years. Those demons are my depression and we have battled for a very long time.

Some people think depression is sadness, and that is a part of it. But it's so much more than that. It's being tired, not just physically, but mentally tired. All the time. For me, that tired comes from fighting it all the time. It's exhausting, because the fight isn't just pushing back the demons, it's holding up the facade so other people don't see it. Depression is also confusion and difficulty focusing. I think that comes from being mentally drained so much. It's like when you're in school and you have that whole day of standardized testing and at the end of it you feel like your brain is just mush. If someone asked you at that moment what 2+2 is, you'd hesitate because your brain just couldn't dig that out. But it's all the time. And because you're sad and tired and confused, you don't sleep well and then your body starts to hurt. It just aches because it isn't healing every night like it's supposed to. And this goes around and around and around in a spiral and then you get cranky because people tell you to just snap out of it because you have so much to be happy about. And you know that, but you don't care because there is something in your head preventing you from caring about it. Is it physical? Psychological? Chemical? Yes, it's all those things in varying degrees for different people.

My depression is not your depression and your depression is not the same as anyone else's. I would never presume to tell anyone I know what they are going through. I don't. Their journey is just that: their journey. Their fight is not my fight and their demons are not my demons. But I do know what it's like to get up each morning and have demons to fight. I know it takes courage and a strength that not everyone has. And sometimes the demons win. My heart breaks a little more every time I hear about someone losing their fight by ending it. I will not be another statistic and I am sharing my story in hopes of preventing even one person from giving up that fight.

First, this is my story. I am not a medical professional and I do not claim to have all the answers, but I have found answers that work for me. If anyone finds this helpful for them, then it is worth sharing.

Second, if you are experiencing any of the symptoms I've described, get help. Not just talking to a friend, although that's a start. But get real help. A doctor, medical or psychiatric, or a pastor is a good beginning. And be honest with them about everything. You are not going to shock them and holding back only hurts you. And don't wait. The world is becoming more accepting of mental illness so don't hesitate to get help.

Third, if you know someone that is experiencing any of those symptoms, be there for them. Not next week, not over the weekend, but now. Right now. The longer you wait, the harder it will be for them to be honest about it.

Last, you are free to disagree with me. As I said, this is my story, my experiences, my observations and my results. You are entitled to your opinion, but you do not get to tell me that I have not experienced what I know to be true for me. Those are my ground rules.

Chapter Three:
Preparing the Soil

"Sometimes when you're in a dark place, you think you've been buried, but actually you've been planted."

-Anonymous

I've seen that quote attributed to several different people, so I don't know exactly who to give credit, but it has always resonated with me. I have felt buried many times - the darkness creeps in and I feel like I'm suffocating. I not only feel like I can't move, I don't want to. The darkness fools me into thinking it's comfortable and I should just accept it. And I have, many times, allowed myself to just sit in the darkness - both in reality and in my mind. It's a dangerous place to be - comfortable in the darkness. But it happens more often than I like to admit. I get tired of fighting it and I just want to let it engulf me, swallow me up, bury me. Depression never leaves me completely. The darkness is always there, usually just out of reach. That's where I have to keep it - out of reach. If I let it get too close, it will consume me again and the battle starts over, and I must find my way to the light again. One step at a time, breathing in, breathing out, until I dig my way to the surface.

The first time I saw that quote, it struck me as an interesting perspective. Maybe I had been planted? Having grown up with a father who was raised on a dairy farm and spent many hours cultivating our large garden, I knew a little something about planting - and what it takes to prepare the soil. My dad would never pass up a pile of manure in the road left by one of the many neighboring horses. He would head out with a bucket and shovel and bring it back to turn into the soil. "Best fertilizer in the world," he would say. If that isn't a good metaphor for how it feels to be planted, I don't know what is. For the seed that is planted, it's dark, you're surrounded and suddenly you realize how much manure is all around you. It doesn't occur to the seed that it needs the fertilizer or that it is strengthening it, giving it everything required to push through the darkness, through the manure and into the sunlight.

I have dealt with some level of depression for most of my adult life. The severity and treatments have varied over the years, but I don't recall a time in my adult life when I wasn't struggling with it to some degree. I think there have been triggers that make it worse, but I can't pinpoint exactly what happened at each episode. This makes me believe that it is more chemical in nature for me. One of my earliest episodes occurred when I went away to my first year of college.

There is no doubt that I had trouble coping with missing my family, my friends and my dog. I know many people do - that is not depression. However, I have never made friends easily and I didn't know anyone at school. I remember watching from my dorm room window as my parents drove away after I moved in. I remember it because I had never felt so alone in my life. Being the youngest of four children, I was rarely alone. None of my roommates were there when I moved in, but it was clear that I was the third person of four in our room and the first two knew each other (matching prom pictures were the tell), and had claimed the bottom bunks and the biggest closet to share. We had our own bathroom that housed a small metal "wardrobe" cabinet, so I claimed that for a closet and tried to get creative with storing my stuff. I had always shared a room growing up so I didn't think it would be much different, but it was. I didn't know anything about these people. I had hoped that when our fourth roommate showed up, I would have a friend. She turned out to be a Japanese exchange student and preferred to keep company with other Japanese students.

As I stood at the window watching my parents drive away, I fought back tears - unsuccessfully. I just didn't want anyone to walk in and see me crying. I was not going to look weak in front of strangers and, even then, I was fighting to keep up a facade that everything was perfectly normal inside my head. It wasn't just the normal "change is scary" type of fear, it was a fear of the darkness creeping in telling me I wasn't good enough for this, I would never make friends and I would fail. I decided to organize my stuff and change my clothes. There was a welcome dance that night and I decided to get ready and, hopefully, find other people in the dorm who wanted to go. Thankfully, I did, and I got through those first nights.

I liked my roommates, one in particular, but most of the girls in my dorm went home on the weekends because they lived less than an hour away. I did not. I had a three-hour drive and no car. Weekends were extremely lonely for me and a constant struggle. Alcohol was becoming my medication for it and I was slipping further and further into that black hole. By the time we were a few weeks into second semester, I decided I wasn't going back for a second year. I had made some friends, but I just felt so disconnected, I couldn't bear the idea of another year. Looking back, there were clearly signs of depression setting in, but it was not common to talk about and certainly not something I would admit.

I came home, transferred to a closer school with the hope that it would be different. It wasn't. I didn't make friends; I couldn't seem to connect to people or events at school and my "roommate" never showed up, so I was alone - all the time. I had never felt so empty.

Some people would be fine with that much time alone, but not me. I am an extrovert and always have been. But depression is a funny thing, you think being with people will make you feel better but being with them is frightening because what would they think if they knew what was happening in your head? I felt so alone that I would have done anything to have even one friend, just one person who cared whether I was there. I began dating a man 10 years older than me. Without telling the whole story, I left school (again), spent four years dating him and six and a half years married to him before I realized I was still empty and still lonely. And, most certainly, still fighting depression. I took my two-and-a-half-year-old son and finally began to make a life for myself.

I used to say that having my son made me grow up, but now I think that, more than anything, he gave me something to fight for. For so many years I let the depression have control and tried to fight it with alcohol, with men, with anything. But having my son and finding my way back to church allowed God the crack He needed to break into my heart and show me that I was worth fighting for. My son needed me, and I needed to be whole for him.

While I'm not sure exactly when my battle with depression started. I do know that it hit bottom for the first time in 2005. A new marriage, several miscarriages and an extremely stressful job that pulled me away from my nine-year-old son piled onto my already fragile psyche and I nearly snapped. Headaches, constant sobbing and complete apathy towards anyone or anything finally brought me to my doctor to try to figure out what was wrong. From the outside, I don't think many people would have guessed how dark my world was getting. But inside, the demons were getting to me and I wasn't sure if the battle was worth fighting anymore.

My doctor did all the routine blood work, vitals, etc. Physically? Not much was wrong…. but mentally? I was as fragile as an eggshell. In trying to get to the root of my headaches, she casually asked about work and watched as I began to shake, my pulse started to race, my blood pressure went up and I could hardly speak. The job itself was stressful, yes, but it was causing me to lose control of everything else in my life. And I was spiraling into complete darkness. It was sending me into a deeper and deeper hole with my demons and I could not find my way out of it. She didn't hold back, she felt I was dangerously close to a nervous breakdown (her words) and wrote me out of work for six months on disability, set me up with a counselor and, of course, prescribed antidepressants for me.

Medication. That is the answer to everything in our medical system. Something hurts? Medication. Can't sleep? Medication. Can't stay awake? Medication. Family history of…. anything? Let's get you on some medication just in case. And I drank that Kool-Aid for 11 years. Several times I questioned it. Was it safe to be on for so long? What about side-effects? I was assured it would be fine.

I do not disparage anyone who takes antidepressants or any pharmaceuticals for their mental health, and I have no doubt that it was probably the best course of action at the time. I was frighteningly close to taking my life just to make it stop, just to feel like I was in control of something, even if it would be the last something I ever did. However, it started me down a path that would take 11 years to get off. I know they say there are no long-term side effects from taking them but there are side effects and I did not like how they made me feel. They numbed me to my life, even if they did mean I still had a life. It wasn't better, I just didn't feel things as strongly. It was like watching my life with a veil over my face. It was all still there, the demons were still there, I just lived an illusion that they couldn't touch me through the veil.

I also suffered from migraines and had medication for those, as well as a respiratory inhaler for what I was told was Reactive Airway Disease. Reacting to what, no one could tell me, but there it was. It made it difficult to be active, something I had always enjoyed, and the antidepressants made me less motivated to try so I just let things go. I progressively gained weight, which made me more depressed and the headaches became more frequent so.... more medication. It became a nasty cycle and I felt more and more unhealthy. But at least I was alive, right? That was my existence for the next two years.

A couple of years later, I was in a new job at a new company. It was closer to home and more pay. They were focused on wellness and soon a friendly "competition" began to get fit and lose weight. Since I had gained 45 pounds, I jumped at the chance to try to lose some weight on this challenge. I had always been competitive, so this was right up my alley. And I did it - 16 weeks and I lost 25 pounds! Yes, I still had more to go, but I had made a start. I lost a few more pounds but basically settled in right there. I kept it off, too, so that was something, but I was frustrated that I couldn't lose the rest.

That cycle continued for the next six years - a little weight loss, a little weight gain, round and round with the darkness and demons and feeling more and more frustrated that I couldn't seem to get any traction. Was this going to be my life? Feeling stuck behind a veil, never really feeling like myself or getting back to who I was? That frustration led to more rounds of depression and higher and higher doses of antidepressants.

Depression can feel like that relative that nobody wants at holiday dinners because they will ruin the party. But they always show up. You never know exactly what they are going to do, who they are going to embarrass, how much they may drink or how ugly it will get. You know the one I'm talking about, we all have "that relative." Maybe they will behave themselves this time and not cause a scene. Or maybe it will be worse than ever. Will someone say something that sets them off and starts an argument? Everyone is on edge and trying to act normal at the same time for fear of what may happen if "Cousin D" decides to act out. That's my depression: I never know what may set it off, how dark it will get or how long it will take to pull myself out of it. It may be hours, days or weeks. Or it may just sit there quietly, not starting trouble and leave when the party's over. The problem is that I never know which side of that relative is going to show up. It just hangs out there in the periphery, never letting me forget that it is still there.

The side-effects of antidepressants include weight gain, loss of sex-drive, and anxiousness. Yes, it is to varying degrees and not everyone experiences them to the same extent, but they exist. Some people are okay with it, to them it is worth it. For some, that cost is better than the depression. But what if there was a better way?

While there is a history of numerous medical problems in my family, there has not been a history of mental illness, unless you count alcoholism which you can but that is another story. Depression is a mental illness. I own that. Thankfully, our society is becoming more accepting of talking about mental illness and I try to be honest with people. And there are different causes for depression. For some, it is an emotional detour when things have gotten tough, life has piled on. For those people, short-term medication can give them the boost they need to get over the hurdle and back to their life. For others, like me, it is more chemical. There is something that my brain reacts to and allows those demons to take over. As I have said, medication doesn't make the demons go away, it just creates a fog so I can't see them as clearly. With a family history that includes obesity and heart disease, I decided to take a long look at my health.

Fast forward to 2014. Like many people, I go for an annual physical. Since I also see an Ob-Gyn annually, I frequently see the Physician's Assistant or Nurse Practitioner. I don't remember if I had met Una before or not, but she was British and had a different perspective on medications and wellness. I loved her immediately. Throughout our conversation about my health, I mentioned my frustration at not being able to lose weight. She asked about my diet and activity level (after having been a certified fitness instructor and studying Dietetics, I knew what I was supposed to do), but I was having no success. She suggested I try something different and remove wheat from my diet. She named a couple of books to read and follow the guidelines and see what happens.

Now, to be fair, the idea of giving up bread and pasta hit me the same way it hits everyone I have ever told about it. Are you kidding??? But I figured I had nothing to lose, except about 20 pounds! I had been on the same merry-go-round for nine years; it was time to try something different.

Let's just say that removing wheat from your diet is not easy. If you have never read labels before, you may not know this, but wheat is in everything! It became clear that this meant eliminating processed foods in general - not a bad idea anyway - so, that's what I did. And, yes, I lost some weight. More importantly, though, I noticed that I felt better, I slept better, I was less moody and had more energy. I was impressed! But then I noticed some other changes.

I no longer needed my inhaler. I was breathing better, my seasonal allergies were better, and I could exercise without my inhaler. I thought, "well, that's pretty interesting."

Removing the processed foods started me down a path of going more organic, more natural. And then I noticed my migraines were improving - they were less frequent and less severe when I did get one. While I had been getting them 2-3 times a month, it had been several months since I had one and it was much more manageable. I started to research natural remedies for migraines, learned what was triggering mine (stress and barometric pressure swings, primarily) and was able to effectively eliminate them! Pretty cool, huh?

So, within a year and a half of eliminating grains (they are all processed so they all had to go), I had removed all my medications except one - the antidepressants.

While I was feeling better physically, I was still going around and around with the darkness and demons in my head. I felt so much stronger than I had, but I was scared to go down that rabbit hole again. Depression is an abyss and I was not sure I could face the darkness and demons that live there without medication. And then something changed.

The changes in diet and medication were happening at the same time there were changes happening in my faith. The clearer my head was, the more I craved time with God. The Bible tells us that God will provide all things for His people and I began to see that when I got back to eating food the way God created it and not the way we had messed it up, I could see and feel Him working in my life. I had a new sense of trust in Him and letting Him guide me.

I fully believe that God can give us a message over and over again, but until we are ready to listen, we won't really hear it. That happened in April of 2016. I was sitting in church one Sunday morning and the pastor was talking about what it means to give ourselves fully to God. He talked about how we tend to trust God with some things, even most things, in our lives but we tend to hang on to control of some things. We will trust Him with most of ourselves…. but not fully commit all of ourselves to Him. He asked us to think about what we might be hanging on to control of and not trusting to God. I clearly felt God speak to my heart, "Trust me with the depression." I knew I needed to get off all the medication - no more pharmaceuticals.

Mental illness is scary. It's scary for those who suffer with it and it's scary for those around us. Could I fully trust God to help me with my depression? A few moments later they passed out pieces of rice paper and asked us to write down, if we chose to, something that we would give up control of and trust to God. I'm not usually big on public demonstrations of faith, but I did not hesitate for even a second. I wrote 'antidepressants,' folded the paper in half and walked up to the front where there were bowls of water to put them in. Rice paper dissolves in water. I dropped my paper into the bowl and watched for a moment as it dissolved into a cloud in the water. That was it, and I felt such a lightness overcome me. As soon as I could see my doctor, I would fully trust God with this.

I spent the next couple of months praying about it and reaffirming my decision to go "pharmaceutical-free." When I met with Una in July, I told her of my decision. I knew I couldn't quit cold turkey, so I was asking for her help. She thought about it for a few minutes and then we came up with a specific step-down plan. We went slow so I could adjust and re-evaluate how I was doing. If all went according to plan, I would be off medication by the end of September.

I knew I could do it, but I also knew I would need her guidance in stepping down from them. Eleven years and I was ready to walk away from them. Scary, yes, but I felt strong.

Una was great! She called me before each step-down to check in, see how I was doing and ask if I felt ready to keep going. I did a lot of praying and even more trusting of God. It was a giant leap of faith, but I knew God would catch me. He had been molding me for this moment for a long time - and I was ready.

Chapter Four: Germination

Germination is the moment when a seed bursts open and starts to take root, when you can visibly see something happening - the beginning of growth. You can see a small green shoot begin to emerge, slowly reaching out to find the nutrients in the soil it needs to grow, to become what it was created to be all along. It is still a very fragile state. The smallest disruption could destroy the entire process and the seed would die right there, deep in the ground and no one would ever know. It happens to seeds all the time and we never know, we only see and appreciate the ones that take root. It happens to people, too, they die without ever really taking the chance to become what God intended them to be....and no one ever knows what they should have been.

This is part of why I keep fighting, I don't want to be one of those people that gets to the end of my life with regrets, with dreams I never tried to fulfill. I want to be what God intends me to be, to be everything he intends me to be without regrets or "what ifs." It has taken me a long time to find that courage, but I don't want to be a seed that dies in the ground, never reaching the sunlight.

Journal Entry - 23 September 2016

My new journal. I choose today to start writing in you because today is a new beginning. I have been working towards becoming a new person - a person without any dependency on chemicals or pharmaceuticals. As of yesterday, I am no longer taking any medication. Antidepressants take 48 hours to get out of your system so today is my first day with a clear head and a clear bloodstream. Am I scared? A little. But a few months ago, I chose to give this battle with depression to God. I know, together, God and I can do anything. This is my leap of faith to trust Him to carry me. I have never felt better than I do right now.

I am sitting at my favorite place in the world - Newfound Lake. The sunrise here was amazing! It was cold this morning, the fog covered the lake, I could see my breath. The rock I am sitting on is still cold and damp. But as the sun peeked over the mountains, everything changed. Suddenly I realized how bright the grasses in the water looked. I hadn't even noticed them when I sat down. But now they are like little rays of light all along the water's edge. And it's warm. The fog is burning off, my hands and face feel warm in the sunlight and I think that's how it is with God. There are times that it feels cold, we see a fog over our life, and we can't see the beauty right in front of us. But if we trust Him, and wait, His light will shine on us and everything will be different. It's warm and bright and beautiful and anything is possible. It reminds me that there may be moments ahead of me that seem cold and foggy - or even dark - but He is there. His light is there, and He will carry me back into the light. I can do all things through Him - and I know I can live without chemicals. No more dependency on anything other than what God has made and given to us. There is so much love in the warmth of His light. How could I ever need anything else?

A dragonfly just flew past, lightly dancing on the rocks in front of me. A messenger. A new beginning, a new life.

And life is good.

****

Journal Entry - 24 September 2016

God is so good! He never stops amazing me. Today, after more than 40 years of coming to Newfound Lake, I finally saw loons! I have heard them many times but have never seen them until this morning. After another amazing sunrise, I sat here on my rock enjoying the peace of the warm sunshine, the quiet lapping of the water on the rocks and a family of ducks swimming past. Then I looked a little further out on the water and realized the lone bird out a little bit from shore was a loon. The beak is unmistakable, so I knew from the profile that was what I was looking at. They are almost always alone so when a second one appeared, I was blown away! So graceful and beautiful! How deep do they dive? They would go under the water for what seemed like a very long time. But the water is getting cold so the fish must be very deep, deeper than usual. A pair of loons, out for breakfast - what an incredible gift on a glorious morning. God is very good indeed.

****

I chose to share those two journal entries because they show my state of mind at the beginning of this journey. I was so hopeful and strong and confident - but I was still a little scared. You see, if I was wrong about being able to do this, it could mean my life. Literally. In my darkest moments, I just want it to stop, for things to be different. I think if you talk to most people who are suicidal, they will tell you that it isn't that they want to die, they just want things to be different. I knew I was risking my life for a chance for things to be different. I knew the feelings would still be there, the darkness would still be there pressing in on me - but I wanted to feel those feelings, face that darkness. I wanted to accept it and learn to move beyond it. I had no idea how I was going to do that, but I was determined to try.

The first thing I need to do is recognize it. I need to see it for what it is - a small part of who I am. It is something inside me, but it is not all of me. It pulls me away from who I really am and tries to convince me of things that are not true. It tells me I am not worthy, not good enough, that I am weak. None of that is true. Connecting with God is how I remind myself of that.

When I was young and someone at school would pick on me, my mom would tell me to ignore them. Now, we are not talking about full-on bullying here; that's a different situation. My mom would remind me that they were just trying to get a reaction from me and if I didn't give in to it, they would stop. Sometimes, that worked, but what I learned later was that if I embraced whatever they were making fun of, it took the sting out of it. In today's vernacular, own it!

Over the years I have learned to own my awkwardness, my imperfections, my weirdness. I have learned that it puts people at ease when you can laugh at yourself and give them permission to laugh with you. It takes away the power of someone laughing at you. I found the same to be true with my mental health issues. I own it, I embrace the challenge of it and, sometimes, I laugh at it. I am not saying mental illness is a joke, it's not. But I took its power over me away by facing it and not being ashamed of it.

I knew that when the darkness started creeping in, I would need distractions from it. When I feel that darkness closing in, I know I need to pull my mind into something else so that the darkness cannot consume me. For me, I know finding the light is key. My distractions are my weapons in this battle. Clinically, they would be called coping mechanisms, or ways to redirect my thought process. I call them my arsenal. And just like any arsenal, you need to learn the right weapon for each fight.

As they say, you don't need a grenade when a flyswatter will do. But sometimes you do need the grenade and I needed to know what weapons I had that I could use to push back the demons. This list is not comprehensive, and they may not work for everyone. This was a process, to learn what would work for me and I would encourage anyone to find what works for them. Some of my favorites are:

- Praying - first and foremost, I pray. I reconnect with God and pray for strength. I am not in this fight alone and it is vitally important that I remember that.

- Fresh air and movement - getting outside, into the light and forcing myself to move, get the blood flowing and feel the energy is a big one for me and I try to do this every day. It also changes the scenery, what I am looking at, which changes my thoughts.

- Music - I am a child of the 80s and still love the music of my youth. There is nothing like some 80s hairband music to change what my mind is focusing on - even if it just makes me laugh.

- My dog - Gabriel is my angel and, when combined with fresh air and movement, he reminds me that I am needed and loved unconditionally. He never says no to a walk and is perfectly content to lay at side when I just need to hold onto something and cry.

- Boxing - several years ago I was encouraged by some friends to join a boxing club purely for the exercise. I had no idea how cathartic it would be when the darkness starts creeping in to punch the snot out of a heavy bag for an hour. It gets me moving, it makes me feel strong and in control and releases whatever is causing the darkness to close in.

- Creating something - I have always been a creative person and making something beautiful and useful helps me bring out that side and push back the feelings of worthlessness.

- Writing - journaling is by far my favorite way to get whatever is happening in my head out onto paper and release it. I always have a journal with me in my purse for whenever I need to stop and just face the demon that is fighting for my attention, get it out and trap it on paper.

This is a partial list of distractions, and usually they work. Sometimes, though, I can't make myself do any of them. Sometimes, I still want to just hide under the covers until it all goes away. Sometimes, I put in a Disney movie and curl up with my dog until I feel better. Sometimes, I need to cry it out, just release whatever is going on inside of me and let it pour out. The important thing is that even when I feel this way, I let myself feel it. I face the demons and accept that they are a part of me, but I do not let them define me. I am not crazy, there is nothing wrong with me. I fight a mental illness. It is a very small part of who I am, but it is always present, and I have to be mindful of it. A very big part of the journey has been getting to know myself and accept who I am. The world likes to judge. Don't let them.

You will notice that talking to someone is not on the list. I don't talk about it, not very often anyway, and for good reason. So often people that battle depression are encouraged to talk about it. There are billboards, ads in magazines, commercials on TV with celebrity endorsements begging you to talk to someone. We even had a poster in an office I used to work in with simple facial expressions on it encouraging you to call the hotline if you felt like any of those "emojis." Most often, after someone loses their fight, the friends and family lament that, "they could have talked to me" or "I had no idea things were that bad." It is most truly heartbreaking, but even more so to those of us that have been there because, while the survivors are left lost, confused, and angry, we know that there were warning signs that were missed.

My mom once said that she thought suicide was the ultimate act of selfishness because there is no thought or regard for the people left behind. I'm not sure that is entirely true. Selfishness implies that there is not any concern for the people left behind, which I don't think is always the case. I know, for me, I think about my family and friends all the time. But I think about whether they would care, would it be so bad for them? Or would it be easier for them without the burden I place on them? Of course, when I'm in a good place, I know none of that is true. Those are the thoughts of my demons penetrating my heart and causing me to second-guess my worth. They tempt me to end my pain and let those that care about me move on, find someone 'normal.' They deserve that. My demons try to convince me that ending it would, in fact, be the ultimate act of selflessness. But it's not.

I am going to be very blunt right here. I have been at services for suicide victims and talked to people after a suicide and they are always lamenting that they wished the person had reached out. I am here to tell you that they probably did. And you missed it. I can almost guarantee it.

You see, people that are fighting this battle are being held captive in their own head. They are chained up, locked in and being beaten down by their own demons. They are fighting with everything they have. Day after day, they struggle to survive, alone in the darkness, alone in their cell with only the voice of their captor telling them to give up. After months, maybe years, they dig deeper inside themselves, find the last bit of strength to make the extra push to mentally crawl towards a door or window, push it open a crack and quietly ask for help. It's not a scream or any dramatic sign; it's a quiet whisper and it usually sounds something like this:

> "I'm just having a hard time right now."

> "Thanks, but I'm not really up to it tonight."

> "It's been a tough day."

> "I think I'd rather be alone right now."

> "I just want some quiet time."

None of those sound like a person on the verge of giving up, and just because someone says those things does not mean they are necessarily contemplating suicide. But the person that is, may say something like that as a last-ditch effort to find someone that cares. They are trying desperately to let someone know they need help without alerting their demons that they are calling for reinforcements. And how a person responds is the key to whether they will ever attempt to reach out again.

I am a fighter. I have said all those things before. I have even told people about my battle with depression, and I have been met with some of the most callous responses. They were not intentionally so but callous all the same. Have you ever said:

> "Let me know if you want to talk sometime."

> "Let's plan a time to get coffee and we can talk."

> "I'm here if you ever need me."

> "I know what you're going through."

"I know exactly how you feel."

If I tell someone that I'm having a rough time right now and I get a response like "If you ever need to talk, let me know," you have basically guaranteed that I will never let you know. You have slammed the door shut on my quiet cry for help and you have given power to my demons because they are now convincing me that they were right. No one cares enough to help me. They are saying to me, "You thought you were being clever, but I told you it wouldn't matter." Once again, I am alone in the dark, with my captor, and he has added another link in the chain to keep me there. And just like Stockholm syndrome, I start to get comfortable in the darkness because it is familiar.

If you really want to help someone, the response needs to be to put your phone down, stop everything you are doing, look them in the eyes and ask, "What's going on? Talk to me." They need to know very clearly and without question that nothing is more important to you at that moment than taking their hand and pulling them out of the darkness. There needs to be no doubt that you are there to help them and nothing matters more to you, because, in my head, everything matters more to people than I do. If you have to schedule time to care about helping me, you don't really care.

How many people would do that? How many people would drop everything, be late to dinner, miss a kid's game, or skip some other plans to stay and listen? What if you knew it was about saving their life? Do you want to be getting the news that they took their life after you had just told them, "If you ever need to talk…" but getting home to dinner was more important at that moment?

Now, to be fair, no one thinks a friend is going to take their life. No one believes it will happen to them, hearing about someone they love ending it all. I didn't. Four months after my second wedding one of my husband's best friends took her life. She was amazing and we will never know what happened. In the middle of spring, she was participating in our wedding and before the end of summer we were on our way to her funeral with absolutely no idea what brought her to that point. Her family wouldn't share details or what brought her to that decision. It wouldn't change anything, we know that. But we like to believe that an answer would provide some comfort. Knowing we missed a sign, a possible cry for help, though, would never bring comfort because it will never bring her back. It's been more than 16 years and I still miss her and think of her often. Don't let that be you. We would have dropped everything to help her, but we didn't know. She never asked us for help, she never indicated she was struggling. We don't know if she asked anyone. So, if someone does reach out to you, quietly, subtly, know they are still fighting and screaming for help. If someone is drowning, you wouldn't throw them a life preserver and walk away hoping they will grab it and just float there until you come back to pull them in, would you?

The last two statements on my list: 'I know how you feel' and 'I know what you're going through' need special attention. First, you don't. Do you know about fighting your own battle with depression? Maybe. Do you know someone else who has struggled? Likely. But do you know how I feel? Absolutely not. No one knows what anyone else's battle is like. My demons are just that – my demons. They live in my head and tell me things that only I hear. You may have your own demons, you may know someone who has their own demons, but you do not know mine.

I'm not saying mine are any worse than anyone else's. I'm saying that no one truly knows what another person is fighting. Ever. And to say you 'know how they feel' is not only dismissive, it shifts the focus from them onto you. It's not about you at that moment. If you want to help them, it needs to be all about them. Don't talk, listen. Ask questions. What's going on? How can I help? What can I do? Help me understand what you're going through? And then listen. Really listen. Put the phone away, turn it off and fully communicate to them that nothing else matters right at this moment. Make sure they grab that life preserver and know that you will pull them in regardless of how long it takes.

I have a close friend that also battles depression. She takes medication. At one point in our friendship, we could talk to each other about anything. But I don't talk to her about my demons anymore. She has her own and chooses to fight them differently. She doesn't agree with my choice to go medication-free or doesn't think my battle is that hard if I can fight it without medication. It's not a competition. It's not about who's depression is worse or who's demons are stronger. But it feels like it. She doesn't ask how I'm doing. She doesn't check in with me. But worst of all, when we get together, she doesn't put her phone down. We went to lunch one time and, over the course of more than an hour, she might have spent five minutes looking at me and not her phone. I can't begin to describe how that felt. My son was home on leave from the army and joined us. Even he was shocked at how little she engaged with us and not her phone.

That moment, something drastically changed in our friendship. I realized that I no longer felt important to her. I didn't matter like I once did. It happens; I know that.

Friendships change, relationships run their course and people come in and out of your life for reasons known only to God. But I think neither of us is strong enough right now to give the other what they need. I want to listen to her, I want to know what she is going through and, most importantly, I want her to know that she matters to me. But I don't know if I matter the same to her and, right now, I'm not strong enough to carry my own burdens and share someone else's. I wish we could share each other's load, but it just doesn't feel like it once did, and I miss that.

We have a mental health crisis in this world because we are disengaged from truly seeing each other. We get so caught up in our own lives, we forget to stop and notice those around us. If someone tells you that they are dealing with a lot, or having a tough time or whatever, don't just offer an arbitrary lunch or coffee "sometime." Look them in the eyes, take hold of their hand and say, "How can I help?" Put down your phone, do not judge them or offer a solution. Just listen. And don't walk away until you know they are in a better place. That is what it truly means to love one another the way Jesus loves us. See them as a human being that is hurting, that is broken, and help them heal.

I think that's why I like to write down my thoughts. It's how I talk to God and it allows me to get the darkness out of my head and see the light again. The key, for me, has been knowing that whatever I need to do at that moment is okay. I keep a journal with me at all times in case I need to write. It is how I always have someone to talk to that is listening. I'm not afraid to say no to doing things when I just need to be alone. I'm also learning to say yes when I know I shouldn't be alone. And, most recently, I am learning that being there for someone else helps me take the focus off my demons and be strong for someone fighting their own. Helping another person is the best way to buoy myself out of my own darkness and be there for someone else. It just can't be the only side of a relationship.

Recognizing when I need help and knowing what my options are have been a huge part of learning to walk this path without medication. I have a support system in my church, in my faith and with very specific friends, and I am not afraid to admit when I need it. I am telling my story, so others know they are not alone in theirs, and if this helps you, then it helps me, too.

Chapter Five: Growth

Growth can be both a beautiful and painful time. Anyone who experienced true growing pains as a child knows what I'm talking about here. But growth can also be an incredible time of learning, becoming stronger and finding who you were meant to be all along. It takes time and patience, but the results on the other side can be amazing.

Growth is all about learning. In New England, we have these things called potholes. They happen every spring as the winter snow and ice melt and create craters in the roads. If you learn to drive in New England, you can't help but learn to navigate the potholes of spring. Some are just little divots in the road, a minor bump as you drive over them and hardly notice. They are an annoyance and nothing more. Others will sneak up on you unnoticed, cause your vehicle to buck as your tire gets caught in it and tries to keep going. You cringe, probably curse and hold your breath for a few seconds while you wait to feel if it did any real damage. By real damage I mean popped the tire, or worse, broken an axel. Trust me, it happens.

Battling chronic depression is a lot like learning to navigate the potholes. They are coming, you know they will be there, and some will be little annoyances that frustrate you, but you move on. Other times, you will hit a bigger one and feel like something has popped or broken inside you and you need to stop, assess the damage and do the repairs. It's not easy, but not fixing the damage means being stranded. Eventually, if you're paying attention, you can learn to minimize the damage. The thing is the potholes will always come. For me, the demons and darkness will always come, but I am learning to navigate them, to deal with the little ones and, hopefully, avoid the axel-breaking ones whenever possible. That is growth.

Journal Entry - 23 September 2017

For a long time, I have felt that God was helping me find who I used to be. I felt like I had lost a part of myself and I didn't know when. So, I had been revisiting and rediscovering things I remembered from being younger. Some of them were silly things - like that I used to like wearing nightgowns instead of pajamas. Funny how just a simple thing like changing what you sleep in can start changing how you see yourself. That little girl who liked nightgowns wasn't afraid of attention; she would dance around the living room and put on "shows" for her parents, singing along to songs from Grease with her sister. But I had become shy and reserved. I wanted to be fearless again.

One year ago, I took the final step off of all medication for my depression. I had been doing a gradual step-down with my doctor's direction but one year ago was the final step - a step off completely. It would have been easy to let fear stop me, but I wasn't afraid. I had made the decision to trust God to handle my depression, to let Him help me fight. I have struggled with it at times, but not given up. The Bible tells us to find joy in our trials. That sounds like a strange thing to do, but I have found joy in my struggles.

Because those struggles are opportunities to walk closer with God. I have come to know they are part of His plan. I am not supposed to know the plan, just trust that there is one.

Jeremiah 29:11 says, " 'For I know the plans I have for you', declares the Lord, 'plans to prosper you and not to harm you, plans to give you hope and a future.' "

The Lord has a plan for me. I know that, and if I know that then how can I not trust Him? I can't not trust Him. He created me. He loves me. And He has a purpose for me.

****

That verse from Jeremiah is tattooed on my right arm, strategically placed so that when I bow my head to pray, I can't miss it. I got it to remind myself that He has a plan, always. It is preceded by a semi-colon. In writing, a semicolon is used to continue a thought where you could have chosen to end the thought with a period. For me, and many others, the semicolon tattoo represents a choice to continue my story when I could have made the choice to end it. Together they remind me to keep making the choice to continue my story because He has a plan, a purpose and a future for me. It serves as a constant reminder to trust that promise, that He will not harm me, that He will give me hope and a future.

I got the tattoo to celebrate one year of being medication-free. One year. It was a milestone that I was not always sure I would get to. Some people don't care so much about milestones, birthdays, anniversaries. But I do. I like to look back on how far I have come, think about how things are different and celebrate those gifts in my life that are still here. I am so blessed for the friends I have, for my family and for my health. I don't take any of it for granted as I know how easily it can all be taken away.

The first year of fighting "naked" was a challenge. I had many extremely low points, but I kept my eyes on the goal - trusting God fully. When the doubt and darkness would start to creep in, I had to summon all my strength to push it back. I had to keep reminding myself that there were things worth fighting for and the people who loved me deserved my best effort.

It was a steep learning curve - failure was not an option. I had to learn my coping strategies, I had to be honest with myself and with others that I was struggling and needed help sometimes. I had to learn to reach out and who to reach out to. Not everyone is able to respond appropriately, and many people just refuse to understand my need to do this without medication. I have actually had people tell me that I should just go back on the meds and not worry about it. After all, they say they are safe for long-term use. I have walked away from these people in my life. I just let them go. I have had to be stronger than I ever imagined to not only fight the depression, but to fight those people who don't genuinely want to understand why this matters to me and support me. I did not expect that, and I was not prepared for it. They were the potholes I couldn't see coming.

I have had to grieve the loss of many people that I thought were my friends and that has been almost as difficult as living without medication. But I learned along the way that not everyone is meant to be in your life forever. And when some people leave, others come in.

After I reached my one-year anniversary and got my tattoo, people would ask me about it. So, I would share my story. I never knew how people would react, but I would share as much as I felt strong enough to at that moment. If I was struggling with the darkness and my demons, I may just briefly touch on it being a biblical reference to help in my fight with depression. When I'm feeling fragile, I won't share much. If I felt that they were genuinely open to the anti-pharmaceutical version and would not judge me, I would give them the whole story. No one has ever asked me about the semicolon. I don't know if people just don't realize it's not a normal part of a Bible reference or if they know what it means and allow me to not talk about it. Either way, it's okay with me. I'm not always sure that I want to admit having looked that far into the abyss that I almost didn't come back. It's still a very raw and painful thing to talk about so I'm glad people don't ask. It is a moment when the axle broke, and I had to either call for help or be stranded.

The reactions still surprise me. By sharing my story, I have found some of the most amazing and supportive people I have ever known. Some people were so impressed by it that it almost made me uncomfortable. I wasn't trying to impress anyone; I was just trying to survive. Then, something incredible started happening. I started to see myself as someone of value, someone worth getting to know, and as someone with a purpose. That has been the biggest change in me. I realized that others wanted to hear my story. They wanted to cheer me on and celebrate with me. Why? God is doing this in me, and that gift is available to everyone. The love, grace and mercy I have found in trusting God is a gift that anyone can have - and then I realized that is God's plan for me. I am to show His love to the world through this fight, through my weakness.

2 Corinthians 12:9 says this:

But he said to me, "My grace is sufficient for you, for my power is made perfect in weakness." Therefore, I will boast all the more gladly about my weaknesses, so that Christ's power may rest on me.

I don't necessarily see it as boasting, but I do believe that by sharing my story of depression and my faith in trusting it to God I am showing the power of Christ through my weakness. Coming to see that has been the biggest part of my growth through this entire journey. Sharing this story is my calling, my testimony, and that has given me a strength beyond anything I ever dreamed of. It has given me the courage to see others as I never saw them before. To see beyond their brokenness to the beauty deep within, to see their story and give them permission to share that story with me without judgement or prejudice. I have allowed myself to be vulnerable to people so they know they can be vulnerable to me. And when people know they can trust you, they will share the deepest parts of themselves and I love being able to receive that. To show the love of God to all His children by loving them, hearing them and seeing them as they truly are is a gift, I will never feel worthy of. But I am so grateful that God has blessed me with those opportunities to love His people.

A few weeks after that journal entry was written, I was taking notes in church. This was something I had recently started doing because I felt like I needed to be able to look back throughout the week and meditate on the message. On one particular Sunday I wrote the following notes:

It is in the place where weakness and vulnerability are met with acceptance and not judgement that we are made family and the power of the darkness is broken.

We have received love abundantly and we are called to share that love extravagantly.

As I have said, sometimes certain things just stick with me and I feel like God is telling me to pay attention. This was one of those things. By allowing my weakness and vulnerability to be seen, I have been able to find new "family" in God with those who do not judge and just accept me. It is a rare gift to be able to see the deepest parts of someone's brokenness and just love them as they are. I have found a few people who can do that for me, and I have been able to open up to them...slowly...cautiously. It's scary to allow yourself to be that vulnerable, but it has allowed me to share with them and learn to be there for others in the same way. I am so very blessed to be able to love those that are broken and not judge, but just accept them as children of God and love them. It truly is a gift and one I will never betray.

Chapter Six:
Pest Control

"Social Media is a dangerous place to seek affirmation, acceptance, identity, and security."

Cornelius Lindsey

We have become a society so connected electronically that we are completely disconnected emotionally. Our thoughts and opinions are reduced to sound bites and empty promises. For someone with depression, social media can be like the lure of a drink to an alcoholic. They think they can have just one, that this time will be different, or that they can just sit at the bar and have water and talk to people. They can't and planting themselves in the devil's playground is only asking to be consumed in the fire. Social media can be the same type of lure to someone like me. I think I can just check quick and see what's new but then hours pass, and I have been sucked into a black hole of opinions, political rants and what everyone is having for dinner.

Don't get me wrong, I like social media. I like seeing what my friends are up to. I like seeing events coming up and, to be honest, I like all the silly memes out there. They do make me laugh. And I even like some of the advertisements and online yard sale groups. I have sold things online and am grateful for that channel to reach people.

But social media is a drug. It is addictive and consumes your time like a virus. It lures you with funny jokes, pictures of what other people are doing and memories of fun times in your past. It's like a slot machine to post something and see how many likes, loves, and laughs you get. But it is hollow – an empty shell. And as someone battling depression, I already feel like and empty shell much of the time. If someone posts a hurtful comment or nasty remark, it hits deeper for me and I feel even more alone. If I respond to it, I end up getting sucked into a fight I don't have the strength for.

I see pictures of my friends and their witty captions about the fun they are having, and I smile. But there is a little voice inside me whispering, "Why didn't they invite you?" I see a post about an upcoming event, and I want to be a part of it, so I share it asking who wants to come with me. I know in my heart that no one will say anything, and I will feel even worse for putting myself out there and calling attention to the fact that I have no real friends. Facebook "friends" are not real friends – nobody is truly friends with hundreds or thousands of people. And the voice inside me reminds me that nobody wants to hang out with a person struggling with depression. We aren't fun.

I post pictures and updates about things going on and pretend that people care about it. And the voice in my head tells me that I could not post anything for months and nobody would notice. No one would reach out and check on me. Social media is hollow and moves so fast that if I stop updating things nobody will care because there are so many other people posting things that I just get lost in the noise. We never really notice things until they are gone. And that is the scariest lure of social media. My demons will tell me that no one will care if I'm gone and social media provides the temptation that people will notice if I stop posting. They won't. Maybe in a year or two they will get a memory on their wall and think of me. The demons inside me tell me that if I check out right now, at least I know that in a year or two someone may get a memory and think of me. Maybe that is worth something? Those are my demons talking. So, I feel alone and lost and want to connect, but social media is an empty connection; it's not real, but it's better than nothing, right? No, it's not. What people like me need are real connections, real friends that reach out, drop everything to see you and check in when they don't hear from you for a few days or weeks. I know that sounds one-sided but putting myself out there is such a monumental task, if someone doesn't reach back, I will just give up on them.

Someone else may read this and think, "But that's how I connect to people!" No, it's how you connect to technology, not people. I have heard that argument a thousand times, but if you can put your phone down and still be completely alone, you are not connected to people. If the idea of losing your phone or even just forgetting it at home for one day causes you to panic, you are not connecting with people. People are all around you – with their faces glued to their phones, checking their social media feeds and fooling themselves into thinking that they are connected with other people.

I have, in the past, put myself out there and invited people to things. I have shared events and captioned them,

"Who's in? Anyone want to come?" I hear crickets. Nothing. Most people might just think that no one is available and let it go. My demons tell me that people just don't want to go with me. On really bad days, my mind will make the leap from 'no one is available' to 'they were going to go but won't tell you because they don't want you there.' Some people will think that is a ridiculous leap, but don't dismiss it. Logic and common sense have nothing to do with depression. This is how social media becomes a black hole for me: I want to feel connected, so I pick up my phone and check Facebook. I see people doing things, I read a few jokes, scroll past some angry political nonsense, and for a few minutes I get to feel like I'm not alone. Then I put the phone down, and I feel even more alone than before. So, I go back to some other social media page, read some more, log out and fall even deeper into the abyss and it keeps going around and around. This is why I called this chapter pest control. The only way for me to not get sucked into the social media abyss is to squash it like a bug.

So, I don't post things inviting people to join me anymore. I might mark something as "interested" or share an event with no caption, but that is as close to putting myself out there as I get now. If I really want to go to something, I will ask someone directly or go alone. It's safer that way.

My last comment about social media will be the posts about suicide prevention hot lines and that they/someone is always listening. You've seen them, I'm sure. It will be a lengthy post about how their door is always open. They will put on a pot of coffee or open a bottle of wine and will listen for as long as you need them to. They are always there. These posts make a dramatic surge when someone famous takes their life. But the problem with these posts is that they lack sincerity and substance. They have been copied and pasted and are a blanket offer to hundreds (thousands?) of people they are "friends" with. As someone who has stared down the temptation of suicide, I can tell you that I would never respond to one of those posts. Someone on the verge of suicide is raw – emotionally, physically, spiritually. They have stared into the abyss for so long that they don't even know if anything else exists. A shallow post online, copied a million times over, will not pull them back from it. The offer needs to be direct, sincere, and personal. Call them, or just show up with coffee and no time limit. If you want them to know their life matters, they need to know they are the most important thing in the world to you at that moment and nothing will pull you away.

I have learned that I must monitor my time on social media very closely so that it doesn't derail the progress I have made. I can lose myself so easily in it and suddenly hours are gone. The realization that I have spent that time allowing technology to lure me into a false sense of worth and importance can send me spiraling into the darkness. The notifications on my phone are a constant pull towards it so I turn them off. There are most certainly some benefits to it, just like there are some bugs in the garden that are beneficial. But too often they are just a nuisance, eating away at the new growth and progress I have made.

Chapter Seven: Weeding

When I was a child, helping to weed the garden was a never-ending chore. I hated it, not just because it was dirty and hard work, but because I knew there were snakes and bugs in the garden. Some bugs didn't bother me, toads never bothered me, although they would startle me. It was the snakes that I couldn't stand. Weeding out the things that would choke the vegetables meant risking finding a snake. They terrified me. Something about the deadness in their eyes, the way they move, how still they can be until you are right on top of them. To this day, I can't stand even a picture of one. I hide my face from them in movies or on TV and have hesitated writing this because it will put the image in my head, and I may end up dreaming about them.

They represent fear to me and it's a fear I have never been able to conquer. Even the promise of a better harvest from the garden if I pulled the weeds wasn't enough to overcome the fear.

Worship Notes - 4 March 2018

The antidote to fear is trust. Fear of condemnation. John 3:16-21

The love of God, expressed in Jesus, frees us from the fear of condemnation. People who live with the most fear of judgement tend to be the most judgmental.

God's love is vast. When we let fear control us, we make God's love small.

God's love is strong. The life and love of God expressed in us here on Earth.

God's love is more powerful than your fear.

God is light, light exposes the truth. Jesus is the Way, the Truth and the Life. God's love is expressed in the humanity of Jesus. He represents what is most true about humanity.

God is so real; He will only meet us where we really are. The light is not meant to shame, the light is meant to expose. When we put up walls of judgement, we prevent people from coming to the love of Jesus. Belief is about following and following is about humility. Will you believe? Or has the fear become so important that you would rather follow the fear?

****

Journal Entry - 15 September 2018

Newfound Lake - my happy place! There is just something about this place and this lake that calls to me. I know God is here. I think I have always known it, that's why I was so drawn to this place as a child. Every year my mom would pack me and a bunch of my friends into the station wagon and we would head to Newfound Lake for my birthday. In all fairness, with three siblings and my parents, there wasn't a whole lot of room for friends in the car, but we would cram my brother and sisters in the back seat, and me and a few friends would sit in the "way back" with the beach paraphernalia and cupcakes for my party. Logistically, I have no idea how everything fit, but we always made it work. We must have strapped a bunch of stuff to the roof, but I really don't remember that. All I remember about the ride was how much fun it was trying to fit in the back and giggling all the way to Wellington State Park.

When you're the youngest of four children, there is rarely time that is all about you. But my parents always made sure that our birthdays were just that - all about us. This was the one day a year that was truly my day - my friends, my choice of food and my presents! Everyone wanted to play with me, play the games I wanted to play and sit next to me when we had lunch.

There was one year I remember that was freezing - a rare occurrence in the middle of July! They were predicting storms and it was crazy windy - the brutal gusts of wind that signal a front is coming through. Now, eventually, that will mean thunder and lightning and torrential downpours that change the hot, sticky summer air to the relief of cooler temperatures and being able to breathe again.

I think we were the only people at the lake that day, which meant we could run all over the place without disturbing anyone - and we did! When the air is that charged with energy, it's contagious - especially to a bunch of kids!

We couldn't go swimming, we couldn't barbeque, we could barely keep everything from blowing away - but we could *run and play tag and hide & seek and laugh. That's what I remember most of all about that day - the laughter. We came to the lake every year for my birthday party, but that is the one year that I remember most of all.*

To this day, I love a good thunderstorm, the way it changes the air and cleanses the earth. It's like God is telling us that we can start over, fresh, with a clean slate.

I try to remember that when the storms in my head start, that God is there, clearing out the darkness and making me ready for a fresh start. I write, and I cry, so He knows I am trying to clear it out, too. I can't do it alone, but I don't have to. Ever since I committed to letting Him take control of it and guide me on what I need to do, I have managed it. We have managed it. Without medication. God promises to provide what we need - everything we need - and trusting Him has given me an incredible freedom. Do I still feel the darkness? Yes, but I let myself feel it because I know I am not alone in it. I reach for God and He is there. Always.

I think that's why this lake means so much to me, because God is here, always. Just like the sun, which I can't see this morning because of the fog, but I can see the light and know it is there, behind the fog. Just like God is always there for me, even in the fog, even in the darkness, and most importantly, even in the storm. He never fails me.

****

Looking back at that journal entry, I have to smile. Talking about storms and wanting to let myself feel things makes me wonder if I really knew how much this journey would hurt. Allowing myself to feel the storms in my head is hard, so much harder than I could have imagined. I have had to learn to see them coming and catch them before they take over. Sometimes, I can do that pretty well. Sometimes, not.

In the book of Genesis, Jacob spends an entire night wrestling with God, although he does not know it is God. He is all alone on the riverbank and spends all night wrestling with a man he does not know. Near morning, the "man" tells Jacob that he will now be known as Israel for he has wrestled with man and with God and has not been overcome. I can't imagine the strength it took for Jacob to do that, but I know what it's like to fight something all night long.

Frequently, the storms of my demons come at night - in the middle of the night. I will wake up in darkness, physically, yes, but emotionally as well. I don't always know what sets it off, but once it consumes my head, it is so much harder to get control of it. Writing, journaling, helps, so I keep a journal next to my bed.

One night not that long ago I woke up in so much darkness, I could hardly breathe. My chest was tight, my head was pounding, everything else felt numb and I could not stop crying. I didn't know what to do. I suppose the easy decision would have been to take some pain meds, wake up my husband and have him try to talk me through it. But I was too far down the rabbit hole to talk, I didn't want to hear anything, and I was afraid to open my mouth for fear of what might come out. Fear. Complete fear. Something I had not experienced for quite some time and I wasn't sure what to do with it. Three years of facing my demons without medication had made me cocky and when they came back with a vengeance, I was not prepared for the fear that would overcome me. I wanted to just get in my car and drive, anywhere.... away from everything and everyone.... maybe off a cliff. Anything to make it stop. But I didn't do that.

In the darkness, I reached for my journal and pen. No lights, I just flipped to a page and started writing:

"I don't want to die I just want it to stop"

I wrote it over and over and over until I ran out of page. It was a frantic cry to God in the darkness, a prayer, begging Him to not let go of me, to not let the darkness take me. I felt like I was falling into an abyss and I couldn't stop. So, I just kept writing it.

"I don't want to die I just want it to stop"

I was trying to convince myself as much as I was trying to convince God, because at that moment, I really wasn't sure if I wanted to live or die. I just wanted it to stop, at any cost.

At some point, I collapsed onto my journal and let go. I let go of my pen, of my journal and my darkness. I just had to trust that God would catch me. And He did.

When I woke up the next morning, I looked at what I had written. My head hurt, I felt the echo of demons and darkness and stared at the open page of my journal. It looked like the scribbling of a mad woman, and that's probably not too far off. But it taught me something; It taught me that I will never completely conquer this. All I can do is keep fighting and trusting God. And that's okay. It will always be a part of who I am, and that is frightening. The darkness will always be inside me, but so is God. I just need to remember that and not let the fear and the darkness take over. When things start to get overwhelming, I need to pull back and find my distractions, find the things that bring me joy and give me strength. The storms will come; they always do. But the storm will end, as always, and the light will return.

Journal Entry - 16 September 2018

The lake is so calm this morning, barely even ripples. It reflects the sunrise perfectly. When I first sat down, I took a picture of it, the hint of pink coming over the mountains. I wanted to capture it, not miss it. But the longer I sit here, looking up occasionally, I realize it is just getting better and better. So, I stop and watch for a bit. If God wants to show me something amazing, I need to take care to not miss it. I watch for a while, in awe, and then notice the fog rolling in: a huge cloud coming across the lake and mountains and I realize it is going to cover the sunrise. So, I wait, and I watch, just enjoying the show. And it is incredible! Just as the fog is covering everything and I think I won't see that moment when the sun peeks over the mountain, the fog settles...just a little, just enough so I can see that exact moment. And I am speechless. Tears fill my eyes as much from the light as from the beauty...and my soul finds peace. I smile and think, "Okay, God, now you're just showing off." But it's okay, He can. I love it when God shows off and I get to be a part of it. He lets us glimpse His beauty and His power, so we don't forget that He is God. And He can do anything.

A moment later I notice a squirrel tiptoeing out along a branch that hangs over the lake. There is something out on the end that he wants. And even though he could easily end up going for a swim, he chooses to risk it. He trusts his footing on the branch as much as he trusts that God provided it for him. I try to get a picture, but I am not fast enough, and he hurries back to the tree, his prize in hand. Then he climbs across a downed tree in the water at my feet. There is no prize for him on the dead log, but he pauses to look at me, to get my attention. And at that moment the sunlight hits a tiny, perfect spider web that I hadn't even noticed. It was only a few feet away, but I had missed it.

My squirrel friend had paused from his treasure hunt of winter preparations to give me my own treasure. Spider webs fascinate me - so delicate looking, so detailed and perfect, but so dangerous to the wrong thing. It all depends on our perspective whether we see beauty or danger. I thank the squirrel for the gift, and he goes back to work. His preparations mean life or death for him this winter and, yet, he paused to share something beautiful with me.

Most of my work, maybe all of my work, is not life or death, but how often do I pause to share something beautiful with someone? Even pause just to appreciate something beautiful around me. That is what it means to choose joy - everyday. To pause and see the beauty, to share that beauty with a stranger, to show another human being that they matter and are worth being kind to, that is choosing joy.

The ducks are noisy this morning on the lake - shouts of joy. I say good morning to them and smile. They choose joy, too.

****

John 1:5 says, "The light shines in the darkness, and the darkness has not overcome it."

Remembering to choose joy, every single day, to share joy every day is how I am learning to keep the darkness at bay, to keep the fear under control. I don't ever want to have another night of feeling like I'm falling into the abyss. But if I do, I know that the light does shine, and the darkness will never overcome it.

We had a windstorm blowing through the past couple of nights. Whenever a front is coming through, the drastic change in barometric pressure causes high winds. Not like the sustained winds in a hurricane, these are gusts of swirling winds ebbing and flowing in a random pattern, blowing things over, shaking the house and taking down tree limbs or even whole trees. Frequently, people lose power in storms like this. Thankfully, we rarely do at my house. The darkness would make it so much worse.

These storms are exactly what it's like in my head. Surges of energy with no type of pattern, causing chaos and destruction and darkness. It can be own personal windstorm blowing through and upsetting things with no end in sight and no way to control it. But, in my head, I have learned it will pass. It is my storm and I find ways to keep my mind on other things until it stops. And I can resume the order and control to keep fighting.

But when a windstorm blows through my little town, it's like the storm in my head has escaped and is consuming me. The pressure makes it hard to breathe, the banging of things against the house is the pounding of my heart and the howling of the wind is my demons reminding me of their power. At any moment they could just pick me up and carry me away and I am fighting for nothing. I never feel more helpless against my demons than when the wind is trying to consume me. And I wrestle. I pray, I cry to God, I beg for strength and mercy and to make it stop. I feel God holding me and I know that I am not alone. He is with me and He is powerful enough to calm the storm and protect me. He does, every single time. The storm passes and I am at peace again. I am exhausted and humbled, but I am at peace. I can go outside and clean up the broken branches, put things back in order and know that the demons will not win.

It is interesting to me that, as much as I love a good thunderstorm, the high winds that so often precede it terrify me, especially at night. Any high windstorm can shake me, grip me with fear. It's frightening to think what wind can do. But I have been trying to learn to breathe through it, focus on what I can control. I have been told to think of it as Mother Nature breathing, so I sit and breathe with her...deep breaths...until we both calm down. It has become another coping mechanism, another tool in my arsenal and it has made me stronger. I breathe and face the wind by walking in it, literally facing it. And, together, we see another day. The storms of my depression will come, but they will also pass, and the light will return.

Chapter Eight: Pruning

Pruning is such a difficult, but necessary part of growth. Prune too much and you risk killing the plant, too little and you don't encourage the growth it needs. I have often wondered if it is painful for the plant but needed to grow stronger. It's not unlike the image in the opening quote of this book, God breaking us down to remake us. The image of Him pruning off branches to encourage growth also works. Many times, the branches we prune are the older branches, the ones that have been there the longest and look healthy, but they need to go in order to encourage new growth. Last fall, I came face to face with the feelings of being pruned, being broken down yet again and remade. And it made for some very harsh lessons.

Journal Entry - 14 September 2019

We were talking about valleys of the shadow of death (Psalm 23) this morning. When is our valley? What do valleys look like? I'm in a valley right now - it's dark, it's cold, and I feel very lost and alone. I am trying to remember that God is still near, He is still trying to comfort me, but I am struggling. There are so many things pulling against me, and I feel like I am reaching out for God, but I can't find Him. I know He has a plan; I know this is just a season and it will pass. But today I fear I won't have the strength to hold on long enough for the season to change.

Why is all of this happening? My mom, my job, my training, everything? There needs to be a reason He is bringing all this to me. I know He will bring me through it, but I am breaking down again. Is He remaking me? Am I a clay pot that He is molding into something new? What are my gifts? What do I have to offer to the world? I feel as if there is nothing to offer, no one would really notice if I wasn't around. Mike would. And Gabe. But even they would move on without me. It's not that I want to die - I don't. I just want things to be different. At one time in my life I had the strength and the motivation to change things. To "put on my girdle and lipstick and get on with it," as my great-grandmother would say. But I don't know how to do that anymore. I feel so beaten down and empty and that I have nothing to offer to the world. What could I offer?

People think I have so much together - that life is so good for me. That's part of what is exhausting - keeping up the appearance. It's a double-edged sword. If I keep up the appearance, no one knows how bad it is. If I don't keep it up, no one wants to be around me. Or they don't take it seriously. People say they want to help, they are always listening, but they don't understand the strength it takes to reach out. And then when you do tell someone you are having a hard time, it's met with, "If you want to talk, let me know." Nope. I just summoned all my strength to say what I did, and it was shot down. I'm not important enough right now for you to drop what you're doing and help me, so why should I try? That is the biggest question that I wrestle with: why should I try? What purpose is there to my life? I want to find that - a reason to keep going. But I'm tired. So, so tired. I just want to rest for a while, to not have to keep fighting. Even if it's just for a few days, I want to breathe. I just wish I could breathe. In. Out. In. Out. Just breathe.

****

The weeks and even months leading up to that journal entry would most certainly qualify as pruning. People and things in my life that I thought I could depend on were suddenly not there for me, like they had just been cut off without my knowledge. But here's the thing about pruning - the plant has no say in what gets cut off or cut out, and it has no idea what type of growth will be encouraged because of it. I was spiraling into a very dark space and every lifeline that I thought I could reach for wasn't there. I was drowning and no one could see it. I felt like I had fallen overboard and was screaming for help and was told, "You know how to swim, get back in the boat." Even the people closest to me, those that I thought I could depend on, couldn't see how I was hurting. It was devastating to me. Was I not screaming loud enough? Could they not see the panic in my eyes? How terrified and lost I was? Had I become too good at hiding it?

When a plant is pruned, those places where branches are removed are very raw, like open wounds. If you cut too many, the plant doesn't have the strength to come back from it and continue growing. If you cut too deep, the plant could die. I didn't die, but the wounds were so deep that it changed how I saw some people, those people who I thought would always be there for me. I was driving people away with what was happening in my head and, instead of throwing me a lifeline, asking what was going on to make me that way, they just left me there to drown.

God was removing so many things and people from my life and I could not understand why. I thought they would always be there but looking back I can see that they had just become familiar and comfortable. I was used to them, and they were used to me always pulling myself back into the boat. But the harsh reality of that time in my life was that they were no longer helping me to grow or reaching out to save me, they were letting go when I needed them the most. I don't think it was on purpose, but I do believe it was part of God's purpose. They were comfortable and I have learned that growth only occurs outside our comfort zone. As painful as the pruning was, and is, I can see how necessary it all was. The way I saw some people in my life began to change and my life would never be the same. I began to see that shift very soon after writing that journal entry.

Journal Entry - 15 September 2019

Today, I am at my favorite place, Newfound Lake, on my favorite rock, tucked down along the water's edge. No one can see me down here, so it's my special place. I can listen to the haunting cries of the loon, the gentle coo of the mourning dove, watch the fog gently rise and glide across the water as I wait for the first ray of sunlight to peek over the mountains.

It's a clear morning, no clouds around, and the sky is already bright. From a distance, you might think the sun is already up, but from my quiet retreat by the water, I am not fooled. I can see the glow concentrating in one spot over the mountain. I know where it will appear first, and my heart starts to dance with anticipation. This is my moment, just between me and God. The loon starts to call more passionately, he can feel the new energy, too. A duck I hadn't noticed flies across my view, and I feel the joy of another surprise blessing that God chose to show me. The glow is getting brighter, more intense, spreading further across the hills, but still He makes me wait. A dragonfly dips and whirls across the water, getting his breakfast but pausing gently to acknowledge me. Nature seems to know that I am not here to disturb them, only appreciate their beauty and simplicity. The air starts to change as the sun's energy grows stronger, but still He makes me wait. It is a lesson in patience - "appreciate the journey and the process" the world seems to say. The gift is coming. As the glow brightens, I think, "Any second.... any second..." But still I wait. It is a metaphor for life and faith. The beauty along the way reminds us to have faith, to appreciate the little things and trust in the gift at the end. I stare and wait. Not yet, but I know it is coming. The glow concentrates a little more and a leaf falls into the water and pulls at my attention for just a second. But I stay vigilant - the prize is coming. I can see every tree on the top of the mountain as the light brings each one to life in front of me. It's that final piece before I am blinded by the first rays over the trees and everything is consumed by light.

And, suddenly, there it is! A giant explosion of light and heat over the mountain, reflecting into a single trail across the water towards me, beckoning me to step out onto it and follow where it leads. I glance away, my eyes can't take it all in, and I notice for the first time a beautiful, intricate spider web in front of me. Without the light, I never would have noticed it. I suspect many small insects have made that mistake and taken their place in the circle of life. But the light makes everything clearer. I notice more spider webs, all along a fallen log just a few feet away from me. The fragile beauty of their trap reminds me that sometimes things that are beautiful are not always safe and only by the light am I able to see them for what they truly are.

The light and the warmth beckon me to sit a little longer, and I oblige, sipping my coffee, absorbing the peace all around me. I make the trek down to this quiet little nook whenever I am here, and God never disappoints me. It serves as a guide and a reminder to me to put the effort in to seek Him, to follow Him, He will not disappoint me, and it is always worth it.

The sounds of the crows and voices pull me back to life, my stomach growls and I am reminded that I need sustenance on this journey, for it is not over. Family, friends and work still call to me and I must return to them, to continue on my path until God shows me His light yet again. He gives me strength, He gives me joy and, today, He has blessed me beyond measure with this moment in His presence.

I pause another moment, not wanting to move from this place, longing for the day when I can sit in His radiance for eternity. But today is not that day. Today, the crows caw-caw at me and the squirrels chatter, telling me to get on with my work here on Earth. Until next year, when I return to my quiet retreat by the water, the memory will have to do.

****

Chapter Nine:
New Growth

After the pain of pruning and the shadow of dormancy, there is new growth. Sometimes, it's hard to see at first but it is there, inside, and if you look closely you may get to see the earliest signs of new life. I brought home a plant one time from work that most people thought was dead and should have been thrown away. But I could see little, tiny signs of life and I thought it was worth saving. I showed my dad and he laughed but applauded me for taking on the challenge. We decided to cut back all the dead parts, which was most of the plant. In truth, it was so pathetic looking that we weren't even sure what it was. By the time we were done pruning, it wasn't much more than a few little stumps of branches. But I could see green in those little stumps, and I knew there was life inside it, even if I had no idea what it might grow up to be.

After weeks of gentle care, we started to see more signs of growth, more green, little tiny sprouts of leaves and the nubs of new branches. We still had no idea what it was, but the joy I felt in saving that little plant was beyond measure. It was a lesson in patience and nurturing - not too much water, not too much sunlight, but just enough to encourage it to keep growing. It took months, but eventually we saw buds of flowers starting and I knew I had not only saved it, I had brought new life out of it that I had never seen before. I don't remember what kind of plant it was, but I will never forget the joy in seeing the little plant that was going to be thrown away turn into something so beautiful and full of life. I have often wondered if that is how God feels when one of His children finds their way and grows into what He intended them to be all along.

Journal Entry - 27 September 2019

I am sitting on a plane waiting for take-off on the final leg of my journey home after a wonderful few days visiting my son, his girlfriend, her two boys and their dogs, and getting a glimpse into his life in North Carolina. He tells me of his life, of course, but it's not the same as seeing it for myself. It is always much easier to fully understand another person's perspective if you have a point of reference from having glimpsed their life first-hand.

It makes me think how much different life must be for those who don't have firsthand experience of God in their life. I have been blessed to know Him, to experience Him in my life and, because of that, He colors everything I see and do. I wonder if, when I tell people about my faith, if my testimony lacks color and depth because they have not experienced it themselves. How can I make it more real to them? How can I help them experience His grace and love the way I do? Jesus calls us to be His hands and feet here on Earth, but how do we do that in a way that can even begin to open up the love and peace that comes from knowing Jesus? I think many people try, and many more think they try, but so few really show the true heart of Jesus. I'm not saying it's easy - it's not. It's hard. It's hard to put aside all judgement and just love people. It's hard to truly live a life of generosity and poverty. It's hard to live a life of compassion and forgiveness, no questions asked. But that is what Jesus did for us. That is what He does for me every day, if I let Him. He invites us into His love, and grace, and compassion, and unconditional forgiveness - if we let Him. And letting Him is hard, too. Nothing about following Jesus is easy - it's not meant to be. Jesus promised us a lot of things, but He never promised any of it would be easy. In fact, He told His disciples it would be anything but easy. He warned them it would be dangerous, they would be persecuted and threatened, that they may even be killed for it. And, yet, they still chose to let Him lead them. We have to let Him, too. We have to let Him lead us even when it gets hard, especially when it gets hard. There is no reward without risk - that's how I know it is worth it. The harder it gets, the more worth it it becomes. When He challenges me, I am reminded to draw closer to Him, lean on Him and experience His grace again.

This is the example we are called to - to let others lean on us, without judgement, with nothing but love, acceptance and forgiveness. Allow them to fully experience His grace through us as His church here on Earth. Again, it's not easy. It's not meant to be. It was not easy for Jesus to take the beating He did, to carry His cross, to die the most brutal death of the time. He did it to show us what real love looks like and what we are worth to Him.

"There is no greater love than this, that a man would lay down his life for his friends." John 15:13

We are not called to lay down our life in most cases, but we are called to lay down the life that this world tells us we should want. We are called to lay down the life of materialism, status, possessions and wealth…. for His people. Sacrifice what the world says is good for His sake? Yes, it's hard. It's hard to live with less. It's hard to not judge. It's hard to accept and forgive the choices of *another. It's hard to trust that it is all worth it, to lay down the ways of this world for the ways of Jesus. It's hard.*

But to quote Jimmy Duggan in A League of Their Own, "The hard is what makes it great."

****

New growth doesn't always look like much when it starts. Truly, you must look very closely to see anything that resembles growth. At the time I wrote the preceding entry, new growth was starting. I was in a very dark place emotionally, but I was fighting. And the visit with my son reminded me that I had something to fight for. The problem was, I was fighting on my own.

It's easy to let the darkness pull you down, forget what matters and just let it swallow you up. It's hard to keep fighting, especially when you feel like you have no support system. Finding the strength to show up every day, not give in to the darkness, to find my true calling has been the hardest thing I have ever done in my life. It meant setting aside my pride, my hurt, and my anger for the sake of others and myself. God had brought me this far on my journey and I knew He would be with me the rest of the way. How could I show people what it means to love like Jesus if I walk away from everything worth fighting for and let the darkness win? I can't, and so I chose to keep fighting. I let my freshly-pruned-self go into a bit of dormancy to regroup and get control of my demons again. I stepped back from training, from boxing, from social obligations and from my family. I approached my job with a confident humility and open heart. I needed to go deep inside myself and find out what I really wanted, find out where I find joy in my life and, most importantly, find out where God was leading me. It was a complete emotional reboot, and it worked.

My church did a series on Following Jesus and what is truly means to follow Him. When Jesus walked along the shore of the sea of Galilee and called the first disciples to leave their boats and follow Him, did they really know what the cost would be? They didn't truly know if they would have food or clothing or a place to sleep, but they knew Jesus and they trusted Him. They believed in Him enough to walk away from their families and friends, their livelihood, their homes, everything they knew and had worked for in order to follow Jesus.

I suppose it would be easy to think that they didn't have that much so it wasn't that much to walk away from. But, if that were true, the story wouldn't really be worth telling. It would lose something if it was just a matter of walking away from a crappy job and lousy little house that didn't provide much. Who wouldn't walk away from that for even a chance at something better? But it's not for us to judge whether it was a good life they were walking away from or the size of their sacrifice. The point is that it was all they had and all they had ever known, and they walked away for a chance to follow Jesus and learn from Him.

We are still called to leave everything behind in order to follow Jesus, but we rarely do. We don't want to give up the things we work so hard for just to take a chance on something better by following Jesus. However, it's not a chance; it's a promise. God promises that whatever we give up in this world will come back to us in the next. Not the possessions, but the sacrifice will be rewarded with security, and peace, and love. We hang onto possessions because they make us feel secure. We hang onto relationships because we think the more friends we have then the more we are loved. But none of that is true. In the blink of an eye, we could lose everything we have – just ask anyone who has survived a house fire or an earthquake. People are unpredictable and can turn their back on you in a moment and then the trust and friendship are gone. Yes, we are called to forgive, but the relationship will never be the same. Still, these things are comfortable because we are used to them. Jesus calls us outside of our comfort zone to trust Him and promises that it will be worth it. That's what I had to do to give up my medication – trust Him.

In the Disney movie, *Aladdin*, there is a scene where Aladdin is trying to coax Jasmine into following him to escape the guards. He frantically says, "Do you trust me?

Jasmine looks at him in shock because the way out looks treacherous, "What??"

He pauses, looks her in the eyes, hand stretched out to her and very calmly says again, "Do you trust me?" That's how I felt that day in church when I made the decision to give up my medication. I imagined Jesus stretching His hand out to me, looking in my eyes and saying, "Do you trust me?" Yes, I trust Him. Saying yes meant giving up my safety net and trusting that he would not let me fall. If I was wrong, I could end up falling so far into the darkness that I would take my own life, but my heart knew that if I took that leap of faith, He would never let me fall. However, just like with the first disciples, there has been a cost.

I have bad days. Sometimes, I have really bad days and it would be easier to just go back on the medication and deal with the side effects. But I said I would trust Him, and I do.

I have lost friends over my choice to do this. Some people just don't understand why I would take the risk and feel that I must not really have depression that bad. I've actually had people say that to me, that if it was truly clinical depression, I wouldn't be able to do it without medication. Oh, ye of little faith!

I have lost friends over my choice to eat and exercise the way I do. They, again, feel like I am being fanatical or trendy or, worse, insincere in my choices to take care of myself and make them feel bad about their lack of healthy choices. Would I like to see everyone take better care of themselves? Yes, of course I would. I want the people I care about to be around for a long time, enjoying life. I do not, however, judge them for their choices.

I make my choice to live like this every single day. I put my trust in God that He created the world perfectly for us to live in and the closer I get to eating food the way He created it, the better I feel. The more I take care of my body to keep it strong and active, the more I am able to help His people and the better I sleep at night. And the more I trust Him to keep me safe without medication, the closer to Him I feel. Feeling closer to Him fuels my desire to keep following Him, trusting Him, and loving Him. He showers me with His grace and love every single day. So, really, trusting Him is the least I can do to show my gratitude.

I have discovered my joy, my true joy, is in serving others. Serving the homeless at the soup kitchen, serving my parents with time and compassion, serving my students in boxing class, and even remembering to be kind to myself. I dug deep to see what it would take to follow my servant-heart. It took a few months, but I found my passion for teaching again, I found my love for the least of God's children and I found that people wanted to hear my story as much as I needed to share it. People like survival stories and I was becoming a survivor. I was changing and, even though there would be fallout from the changes, I felt an awakening inside me that could not be contained. I started to see that God's plan for me was to share my brokenness with others. The more I shared, the stronger I felt, and I began to see how God had been breaking me down again so I could grow. I look for opportunities to serve, to love people and to let them love me. It has become my passion to help those who struggle with life and to see they are not alone. I see them and I love them. And what I receive by loving them is everything I need to keep going. My path looks vastly different than it did even a year ago. There are people who I assumed would always be there that I have let go of and people I didn't know a year ago have become pivotal in my life and on my journey. It's exciting and scary and beautiful because I know it is all part of God's plan for me, plans for hope and a future.

So, my journey has cost me some friendships, but if they were friendships that could not withstand the changes in my life, then they weren't particularly good friends to start with. Sometimes, people aren't meant to be in your life forever. I have come to accept that more as I get older. I miss people that I have been close to in the past, but I think you need to know when to let go. If any relationship becomes so one-sided that only one person is giving and the other is taking with no reciprocity, it has become toxic.

I used to chase some friendships, I would keep calling and texting, inviting them to lunch or coffee, anything. They would be enthusiastic at the invitation but never follow through with making plans. Nor would they return the invitation. That's not friendship – it's just hurtful. When you realize you are the only one who cares about making the effort to make a friendship, or any relationship, work, it may be time to let go.

One of the hardest things I have learned is that even the people closest to me can become detrimental to my mental health. The people closest to us, family, spouses, significant others, are the ones we let into the most vulnerable parts of ourselves. Their proximity to the raw, fragile and weakest parts of our minds and souls give them access to either do the most good or the most damage. They are the people we want to trust, need to trust, with the ugliest sides of ourselves. So, when we open it up to them and it is met with indifference or callousness, the wound is that much deeper and harder to heal. It is a gift to be allowed into someone's heart like that and cannot be treated carelessly. When it is, the damage can be irreparable. When that happened to me, I had to retreat inside myself and make some hard decisions. When I emerged, I was a different person. I was stronger, more compassionate to those like me, and ready to move on to the next chapter of my life.

Chapter Ten: Harvest

My favorite time of the year is fall. In New England, fall means harvest and that means we finally get to enjoy the fruits, and vegetables, of all the work of summer. The planting, weeding, watering and pruning pays off in the incredible abundance of harvest. It is still hard work, making sure that we collect as much as possible of the goodness provided to us for canning, freezing and storing for the winter ahead. It's how we survived as a family, yes, but it was also how we bonded as a family. The shared work of the prior months paid off in the shared abundance of the harvest. But harvesting takes many different forms and the process can seem harsh sometimes.

Not too far from where I grew up in New Hampshire are the famous cranberry bogs of Massachusetts. I'm sure we drove past them on some of our many trips to Cape Cod when I was a child, but I never thought much about them since I didn't really care for cranberries back then. Lately, however, I have gained a new appreciation for how they are harvested. Cranberries take about three days to harvest. On the first day, the bogs are flooded with water right up to the tips of the plants. The next day, giant water reels are driven through the bogs, knocking the berries loose so they float on top of the water, bobbing along and covering the entire surface of the bog. Finally, the fruit is corralled with pumps and conveyors where it is sorted and sent out into the world. Flooding, getting knocked around to shake the fruit loose to be collected and sent out into the world sounds like a pretty violent way to harvest, but sometimes that is exactly how it needs to happen.

I said previously that I felt like I was drowning, but perhaps I was being flooded. Just like the cranberry bushes, the water was right to the top. I could see the light but couldn't breathe. I imagine that it stresses the plants just enough that they start to release the fruit, so when they get knocked around, the berries come loose more easily and start their journey to be harvested and shared with the world. I know I felt like I was getting knocked around pretty hard by the world, but then I started to see and feel the release of the harvest and I knew I was producing the fruit God had intended for me all along.

Worship Notes - 13 October 2019

Jonah 1:1-17

In the face of stubborn defiance, Jesus shows unrelenting mercy. An enemy is someone who challenges my ideals and values. What is our posture towards the "others?" God's posture towards His enemies is love and mercy.

Severe mercy - God brings us to the edge of ourselves and rescues us. In the face of His enemies, God shows unrelenting mercy.

We have received His grace even though we have set apart Him from the rest of our life.

The storm is a severe mercy - at the end of the storm, He shows us who He is.

Being alone - Jesus was alone in the tomb - He would never leave us after knowing how that felt. And we don't deserve it.

****

It takes three days to harvest cranberries - the flooding, the beating by the wooden reels until finally the harvest is realized and the fruit can be sent out into the world. It took three days for Jesus to conquer death - the beating and crucifixion, the darkness and loneliness of the tomb before the miracle of resurrection is realized and the good news is spread throughout the world. It has taken considerably longer for me to become what God has intended - and I'm not there, yet. I am still being broken down, still being remade, still being flooded and beaten.... but I can feel the fruit being produced. I can feel the change in myself and how much stronger I am becoming to fulfill God's plan for my life. The harvest can be devastating to the plant, so much energy and time spent producing its fruit, but that is its purpose - to produce an abundance to share with the world. That is our purpose, too. We are called to share our gifts no matter what the cost. It may cost us friends, family, possessions, pride, or even dignity. It may cost us all these things. But the harvest is worth it. To be able to share our gifts with the world is the ultimate expression of God's love and there is no greater love than that. And as harsh as the harvest can seem sometimes, when left to God, it is never more than He knows we can handle.

One thing that I have learned, however, is that in order to share that harvest, that abundance, with the world, we must take time to care for ourselves. We cannot pour from an empty vessel so if we don't take the time to recharge ourselves, we are useless to those we want to care for. So often throughout the Bible we see Jesus going off by himself to pray, to reconnect to God and refill his spirit. I have learned just how important it is for me to do that, too. I don't apologize for wanting/needing time alone. I make time to pray every single day, to reconnect to God, to hear His voice and feel His presence in my life. Then, and only then, do I have the strength to keep serving and loving His people.

Our society encourages us to be busy all the time. The constant barrage of media, technology, social media and demands of everyday life drain us of what truly matters. For me, feeling drained makes me weak mentally and unable to fight off the darkness. It is critical for me to stay connected to God, to my faith, and refill my spirit to keep pouring out that love that keeps me going. I believe the world would be a much kinder place if we all took the time to refill our vessels and reconnect to those things that matter most to us.

Each day I get up, I give thanks and find a new reason to keep fighting. I am grateful for each day that I am here, and I find something worth living for. I live for my son, I live for my dog, and I live for those people that God chooses to bring into my life that I can serve and love.

I am a morning person; I always have been. I think it comes from being the daughter of a farmer. My dad was raised on a dairy farm and always got up early to get outside in the garden on the weekend. He called it the best part of the day. And even though we didn't have a farm, we did have a huge garden and chickens and those habits of being raised on a dairy farm stayed with him his whole life. I think getting outside to work in the garden first thing in the morning was like a morning devotional for him. It's where he has always felt closest to God. I get that. Being up as the light touches the earth each day is like being there for creation. When God looked at his creation, He said it was good. I see that, too. When I get up early and look out at the world, I can see the good. I see the hope and promise of new things. And those are worth living for.

When I sit at my desk and write, I can see a picture of my son, Michael, and I when he was seven years old. It is one of my favorite pictures of us. I am standing behind him with my arm draped over his shoulder in almost a one-arm hug. He is holding my arm with both hands and my head is titled towards him, kissing him just above his ear. It is a picture of peace and contentment and love. I have no idea what either of us was thinking at that moment, but I don't need to know. The photographer captured that sweet, genuine moment between us perfectly.

I look at that picture and my heart wants to burst. I see the little boy holding onto his mom and think about the man he has become. He is a man of kindness and generosity and values. He has strong convictions and will fight for them. He will protect anyone in need and looks for ways to make the world a better place. He is strong physically and mentally and he makes me proud every single day. I know that if on any given day I had decided to stop fighting, he would be a very different person and I would have deprived the world of an amazing human being. That is worth living for.

My dog, Gabriel, makes me smile just thinking about him. He is a rescue pup from South Carolina and looked like a little Winnie-the-Pooh. I fell in love with his picture immediately. Michael named him. As he said to me, "We have one Archangel, we should have another." We had no idea how perfect that name would be until we picked him up.

Gabe is a mutt, a "Heinz 57" as I call him. They told us he was a shepherd mix, but who knows. He was the only blonde in the litter with deep brown eyes and the most expressive ears I have ever seen. We chose his name before we even met him. When I got to the foster home to get him, I noticed his blonde coloring wasn't completely uniform. He has these slightly lighter patches across his shoulders – like angel wings. They told me he may outgrow them, that they may fade as he got older, but they haven't. At five-and-a-half years old, he still has his wings.

Six months after getting Gabe, Michael left for the Army. I went from being mom to being an empty nester in one day. Parents of "only" children know that sense of loss of identity better than anyone. You suddenly find yourself alone, no one to go watch play sports, no one saying, "mom, what's for dinner." No one saying "Mom" period. The emptiness is profound. My angel, Michael, was off to his own adventures and I was left behind. But I was not alone. I still had an angel: Gabriel. He is the silliest, goofiest dog I have ever had. He makes noises like a Wookie, he hugs me by walking between my legs and curling his head back around my leg, he reprimands me when he thinks I have been gone too long and he never leaves my side when I'm sick or having a bad day. He keeps me on my toes when I take him out because he is a runner and, if he sees something to chase before I do, he will pull me over to go after it. At 60 pounds of muscle, he is a 'rugged' dog as my dad puts it and will knock you over if you're not paying attention. I have to hang on tight. But he is such a lumbering goofball that I can't help but smile when I look at him. And he will do anything to get my attention to play with him. That is worth living for.

The tattoo on the inside of my right wrist, "; Jer 29:11" reminds me of what else is worth living for. That verse says, "'For I know the plans I have for you," declares the Lord. "Plans to prosper you and not to harm you, plans for a hope and a future."' The semi-colon is my reminder that I have made a choice to continue my story and not end it. I need to continue my story because God has a plan for me. It is a constant reminder to me of his promise of hope and a future and that I have something worth living for.

Chapter Eleven: Thriving

What does it look like for a plant to thrive? I think it means to go through cycles of dormancy, growth and bearing fruit. In order to keep thriving, weeding, pruning and harvesting that fruit is necessary. Some plants seem to be lucky enough to be planted in exactly the right conditions to thrive all the time, and some seem to thrive in any conditions. Most people are not like that. We need the constant, tender care of God to keep us thriving. Sometimes, that care seems harsh, but pruning is a part of growth both for a plant and for us. Sometimes ripping out new growth if it is not where God wants us is a part of thriving. How we choose to respond to it, what we choose to produce from it, is up to us.

Worship Notes - 5 January 2020

What does it look like to thrive? A life released into the care of Jesus is a life lived in the care of love and grace.

There are two ways to go about this. There is the life that I build and the life that I release. When we focus on things that don't really matter and try to apply them to life with God, we get frustration. It will never yield a thriving life with God.

Love is a life unleashed! The goal of this command is <u>love</u>. How can we know if we are living a life with God? Are we loving more or loving less? That is the answer.

What kind of year will this be?

A year of building? Or a year of releasing?

****

Am I thriving now? Well, I am loving more and more every day. There are so many ways to show love: smiling at a stranger, looking someone in the eyes and asking about their day, reaching something at the grocery store for someone else, carrying a bag for someone, calling a neighbor to check-in, paying for someone's coffee without them knowing. We call them random acts of kindness, but they truly are ways to show love. And they are simple. Love is not complicated by itself. We make it complicated by putting up barriers and conditions. We look for ways to hinder love rather than just letting it flow. I believe that our best instincts are to love others.

I love random acts of kindness - receiving them, yes, but I love doing them more. It almost confuses people when someone they don't know pays for their coffee or leaves a note on their car telling them to have a great day. And there is an impish side of me that loves to cause that confusion. But what I truly love is knowing that I brightened someone's day. I let God lead me to where and what and I just go with it. And the best part of it is how it lifts me up, it pushes back my darkness and fuels my fire to keep going.

I am back to training at boxing and I love getting to know every one of my students - their name, their goals, their challenges. Giving them a great workout, yes, is awesome - but having fun with them is even better. Teaching, growing alongside them is fantastic!

Serving at the soup kitchen is another way I am loving God's people. I look them in the eyes and smile, say hello, ask how they want their meal that day. I see them. I see their heart and their humanity. I see beyond their brokenness. And I try to let them know that they matter, to me and to God.

And I share my story. I share my brokenness so others will know that it is okay to be a little broken. The cracks are where the light gets in, so if I'm a little bit cracked, it's okay. The light is getting in, but it is also getting reflected back out. I am letting that light shine wherever God leads me. That is what it means to thrive: a little broken, with the light getting in and turning it back to love others, everywhere. It doesn't stop me. It fuels me.

There is a story about two men walking along a beach after a bad storm. The beach is littered with starfish that has washed ashore. One man is walking along, picking up starfish and tossing them back into the ocean. The other man is watching him for a bit and, as he approaches the first man, he says, "Why are you bothering with them? You can't possibly throw enough back to make a difference!"

The first man picks up another starfish, tosses it into the ocean and says, "Made a difference to that one."

I am here, telling my story, sharing my journey, because if it makes a difference to even one person, it has made a difference. And that is worth living for.

Epilogue

So, what are "Severe Mercies?" So often we see things on the news and wonder, "How could God let that happen?" Those who doubt God's existence see it as proof that, if He does exist, He is not loving and merciful. We see the destruction of the hurricane, the charred acres after a wildfire, the death and destruction of war. In the midst of the storm, all we see is the severity. We see the severity and question His goodness without pausing to see what comes next. And what comes next, is the mercy.

After the hurricane, there is kindness and generosity in people caring for their neighbors. After the wildfire, there is new growth on the cleansed soil. Even after war, there is the overwhelming desire for peace. We talk about the calm before a storm, but there is an unimaginable peace, compassion and growth after a storm. And those storms happen to us as well.

Severe mercies are the things that happen to us and seem so unfair at the time. How often do we lament in our own lives, "Why is God doing this to me?" If God is loving and merciful, why do bad things happen? I believe the key to it is in our faith. Deep faith means trusting that it is all part of the plan. Letting go of questioning why and judging God allows us to see beyond the tragedies and the challenges to the deeper blessing within. Trusting in His plan has taught me gratitude for everything I have and everything I am. The good, the bad, the heartaches, and the joys, all of it are part of the bigger picture. Without the things that challenge us, both physically and emotionally, we would never grow, never get stronger, and never reach our potential. The strongest plants survive the storm.

Dealing with chronic depression and anxiety have made me stronger and more compassionate towards others. And fighting the battle without medication has made me brave, braver than I ever thought I could be. It is a hard fight, it is a constant fight, but I see the blessing in it. If this battle is how I can demonstrate God's love and grace to the world - what a gift that is! That is the mercy in it. I don't fight this battle alone. He is in the fire with me. He is in the flood with me. And He is in the harvest with me. He never leaves me. My depression is how God draws me closer to Him and builds my relationship with Him.

So, I have given Him my permission to use me, to break me down and remake me, to fill me with His gifts and lead me to deliver those gifts to the world. What does that look like? Well, in part, it looks like this book. This story is me sharing a part of me, a very deep, personal part of me. It is vulnerable and honest and real. And the best I can hope for is that it will touch someone, even if it is just one person. I want them to know they are not alone.

I pray that you will give God permission to use you. Trust Him even when it is hard, especially when it is hard. He has given you a gift, too, dear reader, if you only have the courage to see it, to use it to bless others. Faith is knowing, even in the middle of the severity, the mercy will come.

I will end this the same way I end my training classes:

Do something every day that challenges you. Be brave and be kind. Go make a difference.

Special Thanks

I would like to thank Amelia Herring for the cover design and bringing my vision to life.

Also, special thanks to Renee Dickerman for the author photo and making me look good.